CAN SNAKES CRAWL BACKWARD?

Questions and Answers About Reptiles

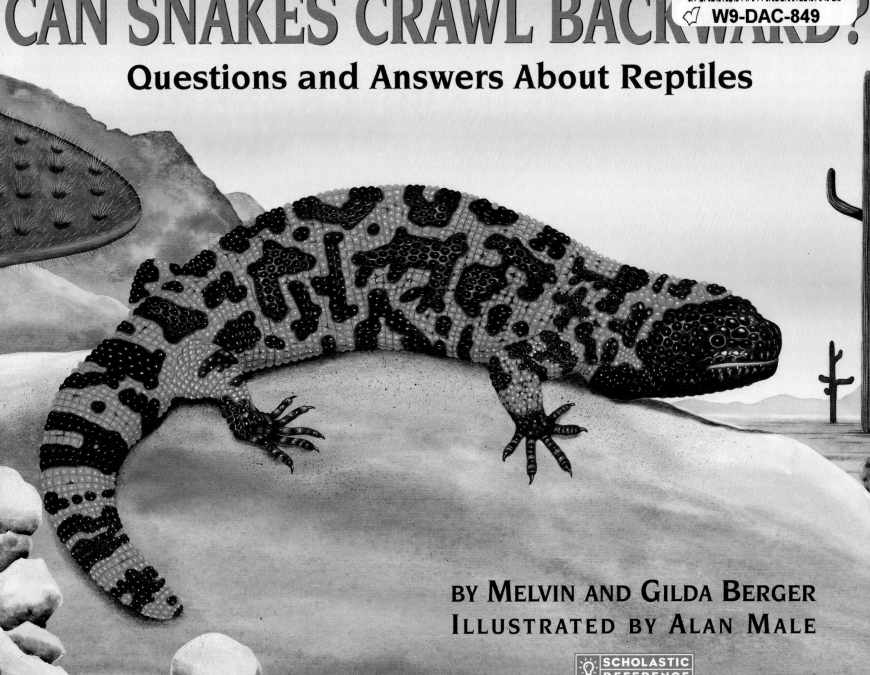

BY MELVIN AND GILDA BERGER
ILLUSTRATED BY ALAN MALE

SCHOLASTIC REFERENCE

CONTENTS

KEY TO ABBREVIATIONS
cm = centimeter/centimetre
g = gram
kg = kilogram
kph = kilometers/kilometres per hour
m = meter/metre
mm = millimeter/millimetre
t = tonne

ISBN 0-439-19381-8

Book design by David Saylor and Nancy Sabato

10 9 8 7 6 5 4 3 2 1   01 02 03 04 05

Printed in the U.S.A.   08
First printing, March 2001

Expert reader: Bruce Foster
Collection Manager
Wildlife Conservation Society
Central Park Wildlife Center
New York, NY

The snake on the cover is a green tree python. The lizard on the title page is a Gila
monster. The snake on page 3 is a boomslang.

For Elaine and Herb, with love
— M. AND G. BERGER

For my daughters, Sophie and Chloe
— A. MALE

Can snakes fly?

No. But some snakes, such as the flying snakes of Southeast Asia, can glide through the air as far as 80 feet (24 m). To move from one tree to another, a flying snake hurls itself into the air from a high perch. At the same time, it raises its ribs and flattens its body, forming a kind of parachute. Down it drifts—until it hits its landing spot.

Can snakes swim?

Many can. Like most land snakes, snakes that live in water form their bodies into S-shaped curves. The rear edge of each curve pushes against the water to send the snake forward.

Do snakes have bones in their bodies?

Yes—even though they may not seem to. Snakes have a skull, ribs, and a very long spine, or backbone, made up of as many as 500 small bones called vertebrae (VUHR-tuh-bray). (You have only 33 vertebrae.) The vertebrae are like links in a chain that let the snake twist, turn, and coil.

Are snakes wet and slimy?

No. Like all reptiles, snakes have dry skin. The skin is covered with a single layer of overlapping scales that are made of material similar to your fingernails.

  The skin's main job is to keep in moisture and prevent the animal from drying out. This is very useful for animals that live in the desert—as many snakes do.

Do snakes sweat?

No. No matter how hot they get, snakes don't perspire. Their skins are watertight. In fact, snakes have no way of cooling off when the sun is very hot. All they can do is seek a shady spot or burrow into the ground.

Do snakes shed their skin?

Yes. Several times a year, a snake's skin becomes worn out or too small for its body. The skin loosens and new scales form underneath.

To peel off the old skin, the snake first rubs its head against a rock or other hard surface. Then it crawls out headfirst, leaving the empty snake-shaped skin on the ground behind it. A young snake may grow a new skin six times a year!

Why do snakes flick their tongues?

To smell. A snake's long, forked tongue picks up particles of animal scents from the air, the ground, or different objects. The tongue carries the scent particles into a sensitive pair of pits in the roof of the snake's mouth, called the Jacobson's organ. The organ recognizes the smell particles and sends a message to the snake's brain. With a flick of its tongue, a snake can find something good to eat, locate a mate, or avoid an enemy.

Do snakes have ears?

Yes—even though you can't see them. A snake's ears are hidden inside its head. Most snakes cannot hear sounds coming through the air. But they're good at feeling vibrations in the ground.

Clap your hands near a snake, and it hardly moves. But if a tiny mouse runs a few yards (meters) away the snake can feel the vibration of its footsteps.

Why do snakes seem to stare?

Because they don't have eyelids and can't shut their eyes. A snake eye is covered with a transparent, or see-through, scale. This eye cap protects the eye from dirt and keeps it moist.

Do snakes have good sight?

Some do. Racers and other snakes that are active during the day have excellent vision. Their eyes are especially good at spotting moving objects. Other snakes can only see well for short distances. Snakes that are active at night have pupils that expand in dim light to make it easier for them to see in the dark.

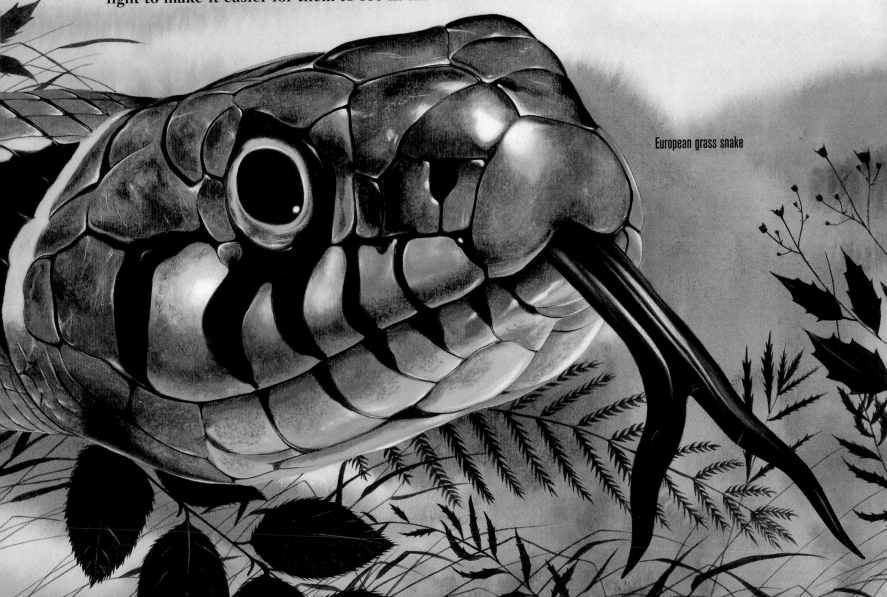

European grass snake

How do snakes catch prey in the darkness?

By sensing the prey's body heat. A rattlesnake, for example, has two heat-sensitive organs, one on each side of its head. The organs pick up the heat from the prey and help the snake to pinpoint its exact location.

What do snakes eat?

Small snakes feed on mice, insects, lizards, and birds. Larger snakes also eat rabbits, chickens, and monkeys. And giant snakes make meals of big animals, such as leopards, pigs, deer, sheep, and goats.

The king cobra is a very fussy eater. It only preys on other snakes!

How do snakes catch and kill their prey?

In various ways. Some wait, unmoving, until an animal comes near, and then they strike. Others sneak up on a target and grab it. Very few chase the creatures they hunt.

Snakes such as boas kill their prey by squeezing the victim so tightly that it cannot breathe. Freshwater snakes use their sharp, curved teeth to snatch and hold their struggling captive until they swallow it. Rattlesnakes, sea snakes, and other poisonous snakes use their venom, or poison, to kill their prey.

How can snakes swallow big animals?

By opening their jaws very wide. Snakes also have stretchy skin in the throat. A python, for example, can open its mouth wide enough to swallow a whole leopard! Muscles inside the snake's body push the prey into the snake's stomach.

It may take a python a week or more to digest a leopard. But then the python may not eat again for many months!

Royal python

Are most snakes poisonous?

No. Fewer than 20 percent of all snakes are poisonous. Poisonous snakes have a large venom gland on each side of the upper jaw. When these snakes bite, muscles squeeze the glands, sending the venom into long, hollow teeth, called fangs. The fangs are like hypodermic needles, injecting the deadly venom into the prey.

Do poisonous snakes bite or kill people?

Rarely. Poisonous species, such as copperheads, cottonmouths, and rattlesnakes, bite only when annoyed. In the United States, fewer than a dozen people a year die from snakebites.

Do snakes spit their poison?

A few kinds do. When threatened, African and East Indian cobras tilt back their heads and squirt poison at the attacker's eyes. If the liquid hits the eyes, it blinds the victim.

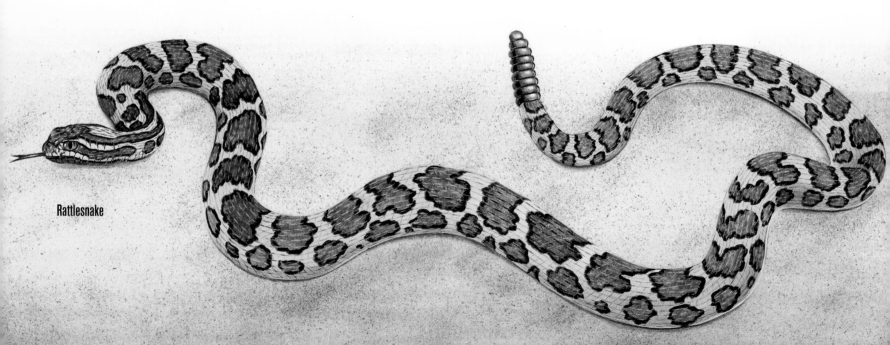

Rattlesnake

What is the biggest poisonous snake?

The king cobra. From tip to tail, this snake is 18 feet (5.4 m) long. Its venom is so strong that only 0.035 ounces (1 g) could kill 150 people! A full-grown elephant bitten by a king cobra will die within four hours.

How do snakes protect themselves?

In various ways. When in danger, many snakes freeze, making them hard to see. Others slither away. Some bite.

A rattlesnake shakes its tail. The hard rings at the end make a harsh, buzzing noise, which frightens enemies.

A garter snake in danger raises its tail and produces a foul smell that lasts for hours. The enemy usually flees.

When threatened, a hognose snake plays dead. It flips onto its back with its tongue hanging out of its open mouth. Many animals won't eat a lifeless snake.

Perhaps the West Indian ground boa has the strangest defense of all. It squirts blood from its eyes at attackers that come too close!

King cobra

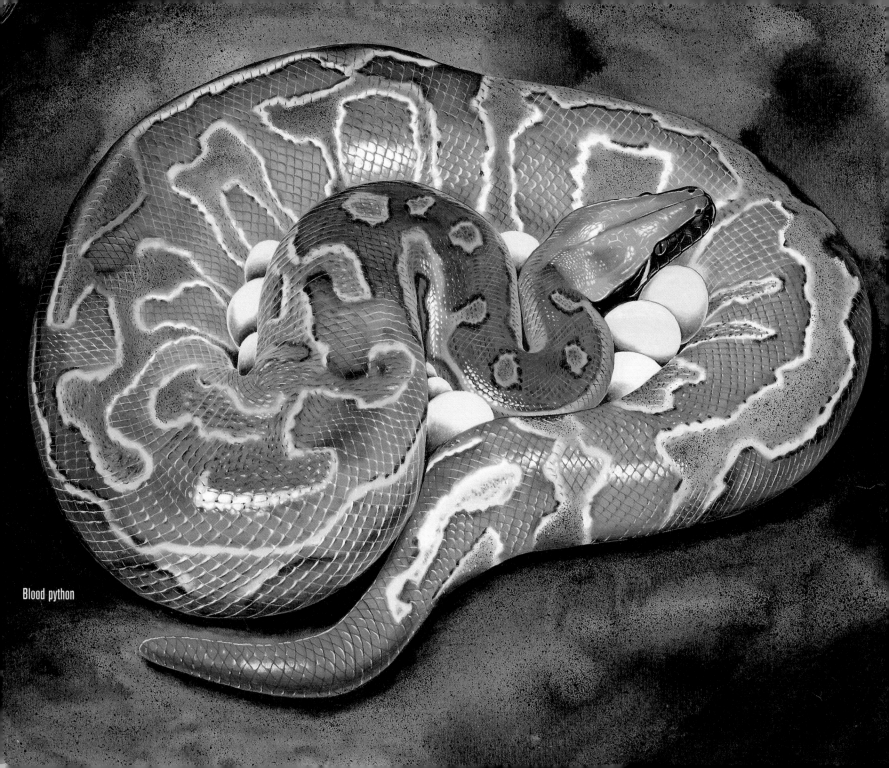

Blood python

Do most snakes lay eggs?

Yes. Most snakes lay eggs in holes that they dig in the ground or under piles of rotting leaves. Within a few weeks or months, the eggs hatch into baby snakes. A clutch, or litter, may have from 1 to 100 newborn, depending on the kind of snake.

Baby snakes have a sharp egg tooth on their snout. They break the shell with this tooth and make their way out of the egg. The egg tooth later drops off.

Do any snakes bear live young?

Some do. Female boas, garter snakes, water snakes, and pit vipers give birth to live young.

Are snakes good mothers?

Not usually. Most snakes do not care for their eggs or for their young. The babies are on their own from the start.

Only pythons and mud snakes are different. They wrap themselves around their eggs to keep them warm and protect them until they hatch.

Are snakes ever born with two heads?

Yes, sometimes. Several years ago, a two-headed king snake lived in the San Diego Zoo. One night, the bigger, stronger head tried to bite the other head, but keepers pulled them apart. The next night the bigger head attacked again. But this time, the heads battled it out and the snake died!

Do snake charmers hypnotize snakes?

No, it just looks that way. Snakes, as you know, are nearly deaf. So, they do not hear the flute music that the snake charmer plays. But snakes can spot movement. To them, the swaying flutist may be an enemy whose movements they follow—ready to pounce. Snake charming can be dangerous!

Is a glass snake a kind of snake?

No. The glass snake is a lizard without legs. Its tail snaps or breaks off as easily as a piece of glass. Like other lizards, it has movable eyelids and external ears.

There are a few other kinds of legless lizards. But most lizards have four legs, with five clawed toes on each foot.

Why do some lizards lose their tails?

To escape attackers. When grabbed by an enemy, some kinds of lizards have tails that snap off at a special joint. Often the tail wriggles on the ground for a few seconds. This puzzles the enemy and gives the lizard time to get away. Lizards that lose their tails slowly grow new ones.

What "tricks" do lizards use to keep safe?

The Australian frilled lizard has a frill of skin around its neck, called a collar. If frightened, this lizard pops open the collar like a giant umbrella, making the lizard look twice its size. At the same time it opens its mouth wide and hisses loudly.

A blue-tongued skink scares away its enemies by opening its bright pink mouth, hissing, and sticking out its shocking blue tongue.

The horned toad lizard uses its own blood for defense. It stands up on its back legs and squirts out a stream of blood from its eyes.

Are any lizards poisonous?

Two are. The Gila (HEE-lah) monster and the Mexican beaded lizard use their venom to paralyze prey. The poison is painful but not deadly to humans.

Gila monsters grow as big as 22 inches (56 cm) long. They live in the southwestern United States and in northern Mexico. They have black snouts and bodies that are a mixture of many bright colors—pink, yellow, orange, and black.

Australian frilled lizard

Which lizards swim?

Lizards known as monitors. The best known are the Nile monitor and the water monitor. When swimming, these lizards bring their legs in close to their bodies. They glide smoothly through the water, swinging their bodies and tails from side to side.

The basilisk lizard can swim or walk on water. When frightened, the basilisk jumps into a river from an overhanging branch and scuttles across the surface of the water on its two back legs. Great speed and the fringe of scales on the toes of its big, broad rear feet keep the lizard from sinking.

What are flying dragons?

Lizards that glide from tree to tree. When flying, these lizards spread out a fold of skin along their sides like a sail to carry them through the air.

Which lizard "dances" on sand?

The sand lizard of the Namib Desert. The hot sand burns the lizard's feet. To cool them off, the lizard raises its legs, one after the other, in a kind of slow dance. If this doesn't help, the lizard lays down on its belly for an instant and raises all four feet in the air!

What is the fastest lizard?

The six-lined race runner. Over short distances, this speedy lizard reaches 18 miles an hour (29 kph). Mostly found in the central and southeastern United States, these rather small creatures—10.5 inches (27 cm) long—scoot away at the first hint of danger.

One day you may wish to see lizards run. You could visit the city of Lovington, New Mexico, on July 4 for the annual World's Greatest Lizard Race.

Flying
dragons

What is the world's largest lizard?

The Komodo dragon. One such lizard in the St. Louis Zoo measured 10 feet, 2 inches (3.1 m) long—the length of a car. It weighed 365 pounds (165.6 kg)—the weight of two adult men.

Komodo dragons live on Komodo Island and other small islands of Indonesia. They hunt alone and prey on big animals such as wild pigs and deer. They lie in wait and then pounce, grabbing victims with their sharp teeth.

What is the world's smallest lizard?

The Virgin Islands gecko. Less than 0.7 inches (18 mm) long, this tiny creature can fit on a nickel!

The Virgin Islands gecko is smaller than a nickel.

Komodo dragons

Can lizards change their skin color?

Some can. Chameleons (kuh-MEEL-yuns) and some other lizards change color by moving colored cells in the upper layers of their skin. The color usually blends in with their surroundings and provides good camouflage.

The color may also show the lizard's mood. An angry chameleon, for example, turns black. Green tells you it is calm. The loser in a fight turns yellow.

Are chameleons good hunters?

Excellent ones. When a bug lands near a chameleon, the lizard shoots out its incredibly long tongue. Snap! The chameleon catches the bug on its tongue's sticky tip and reels it in for a tasty meal!

Double-banded chameleon

Cape chameleon

Common chameleon

Can lizards climb trees?

Some can. Geckos, for example, are good climbers. Most have claws and tiny hooked hairs on their toes that cling like Velcro to flat surfaces. Gecko pads work so well that these lizards can walk up smooth walls and scamper across ceilings with ease!

Which lizard spends all its time in trees?

The emerald tree skink. It almost never comes down from the trees in Indonesia that are its home. Other species of skinks, however, live on the ground or underground. Altogether, there are more than 900 different kinds of skinks. Most live in warm and tropical regions of the world, such as Australia, Africa, and the islands of the western Pacific Ocean.

How did the gecko get its name?

From the sound it makes—"gecko, gecko, gecko"—as it clicks its tongue. Geckos are night creatures that can keep people awake with their noisy chirping and clacking. But people in Asia like to have these little lizards in their homes. Some believe that a gecko barking when a baby is born signals good luck.

What are tuataras?

Two small groups of animals that are related to lizards. Tuataras (too-uh-TAH-ruhs) are found only on a few islands off the coast of New Zealand. They grow to be about 2 feet (60 cm) long and feed mostly on insects, snails, birds, and small reptiles.

Tuataras are unique. They don't mate until they are about 20 years old. The female carries as many as 15 eggs in her body for nearly a year before laying the eggs. And it takes more than a year for the eggs to hatch!

Mediterranean geckos

CROCODILES AND ALLIGATORS

How are crocodiles like alligators?

They're almost look-alikes. Both have narrow, torpedo-shaped bodies, rough skin, short legs, and long tails. All crocodiles and alligators live in warm climates. They're found in or near freshwater lakes, rivers, swamps, and saltwater oceans.

Because they are similar, scientists group crocodiles, alligators, and the closely related gavials together as crocodilians. Large crocodilians slam their jaws shut with a force of many tons (tonnes)! For comparison, you bite with a force of only 40 pounds (18.1 kg). But the muscles used to open their jaws are quite weak. A strong person can easily hold a crocodilian's mouth shut.

How can you tell crocodiles from alligators?

It's easy. A crocodile has a narrow, pointed snout compared to an alligator, whose snout is broad and round.

When a crocodile closes its mouth, an extra-long tooth on each side pokes outside its upper jaw. But none of an alligator's lower teeth show when it shuts its mouth.

Crocodiles are also faster and more fierce than alligators. They prowl around looking for animals to grab and eat. Alligators mostly rest in the water waiting for prey.

Crocodiles are found around the world. Alligators are only found in the southern United States and China.

How long have crocodilians been on Earth?

About 200 million years. Crocodilians evolved from the same group of reptiles as the dinosaurs. The largest, *Deinosuchus,* was twice as long as crocodilians today.

American alligator

Esturine crocodile

Nile crocodile

Which crocodile did ancient Egyptians worship?

The huge Nile crocodile. Ancient Egyptians considered this animal a form of the god Sobek. Nearly 4,000 years ago, people built a temple in the city of Ombros to glorify Sobek. Special pools held the sacred crocodiles. When one died, the priests mummified its body so it would last forever.

Are crocodilians good swimmers?

Yes. Long, powerful tails, webbed feet, and streamlined bodies let crocodilians swim much faster than they can move on land.

In some ways, crocodilians are like submarines. They can float low in the water, with nothing showing except their eyes and nostrils. Animals they feed on don't even know they're there—until it's too late!

Also, when crocodilians dive, special flaps seal off their nostrils and ears. A third eyelid protects their eyes underwater, just like a pair of swim goggles. And a wide flap in the back of the throat closes shut so they don't choke when pulling an animal underwater.

How long can crocodilians stay underwater?

More than an hour. When underwater, a crocodilian's heart beats more slowly and its body uses less oxygen.

Why do crocodilians swallow pebbles?

For two reasons. First, the pebbles weigh them down in the water, so they can float with only their eyes and nostrils sticking up. And second, pebbles crush and grind food in the crocodilians' stomachs, helping the animals digest what they swallow. In some crocodilians, scientists have even found partially digested pieces of steel!

What animals do crocodilians eat?

Any that come in or near the water. Small and young crocodilians feed on insects, fish, small mammals, turtles, and birds. Large adults attack lions, tigers, and antelopes.

Occasionally, crocodilians assault people. In Africa, crocodiles kill more people than lions do.

What animals *don't* crocodiles eat?

Small birds called plovers. Plovers ride on the crocodile's back, feeding on parasites they find on the scaly skin. From time to time, the birds hop inside the crocodile's open mouth. Like toothpicks, they peck out morsels of food they find between the crocodile's teeth. How daring!

What are crocodile tears?

Showing sadness without feeling it. People used to think that crocodiles shed tears while eating prey. So "crocodile tears" came to mean fake sorrow, like pretending to cry when school closes for vacation.

Do crocodilians chew their food?

No. Alligators and crocodiles swallow small prey in one gulp. They rip apart larger prey by holding it with their teeth while twisting and spinning in the water. When one crocodilian kills a large animal, as many as 40 others may join in the meal.

How often do crocodilians eat?

About 50 times a year. Compare that with the 1,000 meals that you eat!

Crocodilians store fat in their tails and in other places in their bodies. They can live on this fat for long periods of time.

Yellow-billed stork

Nile crocodile

Plover

Kudu antelope

Nile crocodile

Do crocodilians smile?

No—although it sometimes looks that way. When crocodilians seem to smile, they're actually cooling down by letting heat escape through their mouths.

Do crocodilians "talk"?

Yes. Crocodilians are the only reptiles that can make vocal sounds. During the mating season, they bellow loudly to warn away rivals. The sound is most like a lion's roar or a badly played French horn.

Crocodilians also rest their lower jaws on top of the water and slap down their upper jaws. That makes a loud pop and a big splash. Experts think it is the crocodilians' way of saying, "Watch out. I'm mighty strong!"

Which is the biggest reptile?

The saltwater crocodile of Asia and Australia. Before the 1960s, people reported huge animals that grew to about 26 feet (8 m)— the distance across a standard soccer goal. Today, the average length of most saltwater crocodiles is between 10 and 12 feet (3 and 3.7 m). Not exactly small!

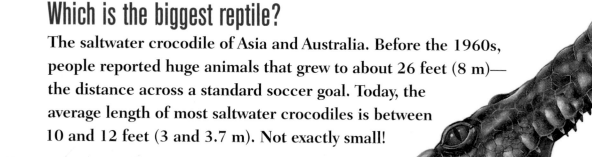

Nile crocodile

Nile crocodile

Are crocodilians egg layers?

Yes. Like most reptiles, crocodilians lay eggs that look like chicken eggs but are bigger and have a harder shell. Females usually lay about 60 to 70 eggs at one time.

Some species dig shallow pits in the sand and bury their eggs. Others hide their eggs in nests of dead leaves and grass. The decaying plants give off heat that helps keep the eggs warm. If the eggs get too warm, the mother may splash them with cool water.

Are crocodilians good mothers?

Yes. Female crocodilians guard their eggs from attack by hungry birds and other animals. When ready to hatch, the hatchling may crack open the shell with its little egg tooth. Often, though, the mother hears cries from inside the eggs. This signals her to uncover the nest, crack open the eggs, and let out the babies.

Soon after the hatchlings are born, they crawl into the mother's open mouth. She carries them gently to the water, where she opens her mouth and out they crawl.

How big are baby crocodilians?

Not very big. Newborns are only about 10 inches (25.4 cm) long. But they grow very fast. In two years they triple their size. If you grew that fast you would have been 5 feet (1.5 m) tall at age two!

Do crocodilians live long?

Yes. In general, the larger the crocodilian, the longer it lives. Big Nile and saltwater crocodiles reach an average age of 70. A crocodile in a Russian zoo attained the ripe old age of 110!

Alligators don't usually live as long as crocodiles. The oldest American alligator on record only survived about 66 years.

Nile crocodile
hatchlings

Water buffalo

Zebra

Sable antelope

Kudu antelope

What part do crocodilians play in the food chain?

A vital one. Crocodilians help plants to grow when they deposit their droppings in the water. The droppings help feed the water plants, which are then eaten by fish. By deepening water holes on land, crocodilians provide valuable sources of water for other kinds of animals to use during periods of drought. Also, these powerful swimmers open paths through tangled underwater plant growths for other creatures that live in freshwater. Without crocodilians, freshwater life would suffer.

Why do crocodilians need help?

Because some are endangered animals, threatened with disappearing forever. The three species of crocodiles threatened with extinction include the American crocodile, the Cuban crocodile, and the Nile crocodile.

People are destroying the habitats of these animals. They are filling in the bodies of water with sand and dirt. On the filled-in land, they are building houses and roads. Without their habitats, the crocodilians cannot survive.

Also, hunters are killing alligators and crocodiles in great numbers for their skins. Manufacturers are using these skins to make shoes, belts, and handbags. Because of the overhunting, the number of crocodilians in the wild is way down.

What can save the crocodiles?

Laws and conservation programs. Since the Endangered Species Act of 1973 was passed, the number of alligators, for example, has gone up. But even more strict enforcement is needed.

Also, some zoos and researchers in other places are breeding crocodilians. These scientists gather the eggs and hatch them in incubators. Then they release the young into the wild. These programs, among many others, are helping to save some animals.

TURTLES

Why do turtles have shells?

For protection. A turtle's shell is like a suit of armor. When threatened, most turtles can quickly pull their heads back inside their shells. The shell is also the turtle's skeleton. All shells have the same three parts: the top, or carapace (KAR-uh-pays); the belly cover, or plastron (PLAS-trun); and the bridge, which connects the two.

What turtle can completely close its shell?

The box turtle. This land turtle has a round, high-domed carapace and a plastron with a hinge between its front and rear parts. A frightened box turtle pulls its head, legs, and tail into its shell and slams the carapace and plastron together. The shell forms a tight box with the turtle safely inside.

How strong is a turtle's shell?

Very strong. Yet it can be broken. Sometimes large birds, such as eagles and vultures, snatch turtles with their claws. Flying high, the birds then drop the turtles, smashing their shells and killing them. A turtle cannot live without its shell.

Are turtles, tortoises, and terrapins different animals?

No. Scientists call all animals with shells turtles—and so will we.

People, however, often use the word *turtles* for animals with shells that live in the sea, *tortoises* for shelled animals that live on land, and *terrapins* for those found in freshwater. Altogether, there are fewer than 300 different kinds of turtles.

Eastern box turtles only grow to be 7 inches (18 cm) long.
This one is larger than life-size.

Eastern box turtle

How long have turtles been on Earth?

More than 200 million years! Turtles were swimming in the ocean when dinosaurs inhabited Earth. And they are still here, some 65 million years after the last dinosaur died. Turtles are probably the most ancient of all reptiles.

Where do turtles live?

Most everywhere—on land and in water. But because they are cold-blooded, turtles cannot live where it is cold year-round. Turtles that live in warm climates with cold winters hibernate underground or in the water.

How old was the oldest turtle?

At least 152 years old. A soldier found a fully grown Marion's tortoise in 1766 and took it to his camp. In 1918, the turtle fell off a ledge and was killed. No one knows how old it was when found or how much longer it might have lived.

Do turtles have teeth?

No. But most turtles have sharp, horny beaks that rip, tear, and cut their food. Alligator snapping turtles are particularly fierce. One bite from their beak could easily cut a big fish in half!

What do turtles eat?

Various foods, from insects, frogs, and fish to fruit, flowers, and other plant material. The African helmeted turtle also eats birds. The turtle sits at the edge of a pool. When a small bird hops over for a drink, the turtle whips out its head and grasps the unlucky creature in its beak.

Alligator snapping turtle

Australian
snake-necked turtle

Which turtle has a trunk for a nose?

The Chinese softshell turtle. At the tip of its head is a tiny, elephant-like trunk with nostrils at the end. Swimming underwater in rivers or lakes, the turtle raises its trunk above the surface to breathe the air. The trunk works much like a skin diver's snorkel.

How does the African pancake tortoise escape enemies?

It hides in rocks. If an enemy comes near, the small, flat African pancake tortoise slides into a crack in the rock and puffs itself up. The turtle cannot be pulled out!

Which turtle smells bad?

The stinkpot turtle. It lets out a foul and terrible odor that drives away its enemies—fast. Stinkpot turtles also have strong jaws to bite animals not bothered by their smell.

What colors are painted turtles?

Their heads are usually olive green, with bright yellow or red stripes. Most have vivid red markings on their dark carapaces. The plastrons are either yellow or yellow with dark lines.

Oddly enough, young and old painted turtles eat different foods. Young ones make meals of bugs, tadpoles, and other water creatures. Older painted turtles consume plants growing in the water.

Which turtle has a neck like a snake?

The Australian snake-necked turtle. This reptile lives in ponds, lakes, and swamps. It catches small fish and tadpoles by whipping out its long, skinny neck and grabbing them in its beak.

But its neck is too long to fit inside its shell. So the turtle folds its neck to the side and tucks it under the edge of its carapace.

Which islands were named after a turtle?

The Galápagos (guh-LAH-puh-gohs) Islands, 600 miles (965 km) off the coast of Ecuador in South America. The Spanish word *galápagos* is also the name of the huge turtles that live on the islands. Experts believe the turtles originally floated to the islands from the coast of South America on big pieces of driftwood.

Galápagos turtles, or tortoises, are among the world's largest land turtles. The average Galápagos turtle is about one-half the length and weight of a very small car! One in Seffner, Florida, weighs 911 pounds (413.2 kg) and measures 54 inches (137 cm) in length.

How do zoo doctors give Galápagos turtles their medicine?

They hide it in tomatoes. Veterinarians have found that Galápagos turtles will eat almost anything that is red. So they put their pills inside red tomatoes!

Giant Galápagos turtles

Which is the biggest turtle?

A sea turtle called the leatherback. As you can probably guess, it has a leathery skin covering its shell. One found dead on a beach in 1988 was 9 feet, 5 inches (2.9 m) long and weighed an astonishing 2,120 pounds (961.6 kg)!

In the warm ocean waters around the world where it lives, the leatherback swims at about 22 miles an hour (35.4 kph). A fast human swimmer can't do more than 12 miles an hour (19.3 kph).

Do sea turtles breathe air?

Yes. Like other reptiles, turtles that live in the sea breathe air. When swimming, they have to come up to the surface every 5 or 10 minutes. But if they're just resting on the ocean floor, they can go for hours without taking a breath.

Leatherback turtle

Which turtle lays the most eggs?

The green sea turtle. The female of this species is like all sea turtles. She swims to the beach where she was born to lay her eggs. With great difficulty she drags herself onto the sand. The turtle then digs a hole with her back flippers and deposits as many as 100 eggs. She covers the eggs and then lumbers back into the water. Before summer is over, she may return several times—and lay more than 1,000 eggs in all!

Do sea turtles cry when laying eggs?

No—even though it looks that way. When sea turtles lay their eggs, tears seem to stream from their eyes. The tears are saltwater from their bodies that flows out while the turtles are nesting to help keep sand out of their eyes.

When do the eggs hatch?

In about two months. Hatchlings dig their way out of their nest and wait for dark to head for the water. But even so, they're hardly safe. Along the way, many are caught and eaten by gulls, crabs, rats, and foxes.

How do people harm sea turtles?

In many ways. Dune buggy tires crush the sea turtles' nests and hatchlings. Sometimes the tiny turtles fall into deep tire ruts and can't crawl out.

Plastic garbage dumped into the oceans also hurts sea turtles. The turtles often mistake floating plastic bags for jellyfish and swallow them. If the plastic blocks a turtle's throat it will starve to death.

Other forms of pollution, such as oil, tar, and poisonous chemicals, are also dangerous, especially to young turtles.

This Kemp's ridley sea turtle is preparing a nest for her eggs.

Have any turtles become extinct?

Some types have. The Kemp's ridley turtle is nearly extinct, and other sea turtles are endangered. Some land turtles, like the bog turtle, are endangered, too. Once gone, these turtles will never come back.

What's the best way to enjoy reptiles?

Follow these rules:

- Don't harm any reptiles you find.
- Save small reptiles you find on roadways by lifting them out of harm's way—but keep a safe distance from those that might be poisonous or otherwise dangerous.
- Help to protect and clean up the land and water where reptiles live.
- Ask elected officials to pass laws against catching sea turtles in large fishing nets.
- Respect reptiles. Do not take them home to keep as pets. Enjoy reptiles where you find them!

Kemp's ridley sea turtles

INDEX

About the Authors

Each spring the Bergers eagerly look forward to visits from Eastern box turtles in their neighborhood. Their love for the turtles makes them very concerned about the many wild reptiles that must struggle to survive. "If reptiles are going to be around for another 100 million years," they say, "we've got to help them!"

About the Illustrator

Alan Male lives with his family in Cornwall, England, and has worked as an illustrator for many years. "I enjoy drawing reptiles because they have interesting colors, textures, and shapes," he says.